The Short Cheap Tax Book for the Trump/GOP Tax Law

A bunch of things that everyone should know about the new law

2019 Revision

By Kirk Taylor

How This Book Works

This book is designed to give a quick overview of the changes in the tax bill that was just signed into law by President Trump. I'm attempting to explain things for the most part in plain English when possible. The book is going to try to give advice on what you can do to set yourself up for success in this brave new world. The new law changes A LOT, but not as much as what we were expecting.

UPDATE: Contrary to the next paragraph, the book was updated in January 2019 to have the latest information on proposed and approved regulations, as well as interpretations. Much of the law has not been litigated in court, so there is some lack of certainty about the more nuanced points, but most of the information is much more reliable than when the book was originally published.

I'm writing this within days of reading the bill (dozens of times) so some of the chapters may tell you to be careful using the advice. I will update the book as I find errors or reinterpretations. For those of you who have already bought the book, a list of corrections will be maintained on my blog, linked below. Check regularly to see what I messed up (5 errors corrected so far – all mostly minor):

http://supertaxgenius.blogspot.com/2017/12/book-owner-exclusives.html

This book is not comprehensive and doesn't cover all the changes. It covers areas that I think are applicable to most people and covers areas in various levels of detail depending on how many people I think they apply to, or whether I can cover them adequately in this type of book. Don't assume that just because I didn't talk about something that it wasn't affected by the bill. One of the first chapters will cover all the things that were discussed or passed by one or another of the chambers of Congress that didn't actually make it into the final bill.

This book is cheapest when read on a Kindle, and the links will function best there as well. If you don't have a Kindle, amazon has a free, downloadable app for cell phones, and a cloud reader for reading on your laptop or home computer. If you have a print version, lines may be skewed due to long links messing up the formatting – sorry. Anyway, for best results, read the whole book – it's short!

One convention to be aware of: The first time in a chapter that I use a term that will be repeated, I will often put an abbreviation in parenthesis after it so you know what I mean later. For example, As Soon As Possible (ASAP) tells you what ASAP means when I use it later. I will use this a lot for the five filing statuses: Married Filing Jointly (MFJ), Married Filing Separately (MFS), Head of Household (HH), Single (S) and Qualifying Widower (QW).

Some things that are eliminated are actually "suspended" mostly through 2025 or 2026. I refer to them as cancelled or eliminated because who knows what will happen between now and then. For all intents and purposes, they are gone forever in the world of partisan politics and divisive government.

If a chapter has a "Read the Bill" link. It links to the conference agreement discussion of the changes, which comes after the actual text of the bill. It is in English, starts with an explanation of current law, then gives the House and Senate proposals, and then tells you what was agreed to. It's a great way to understand what changed by understanding the law as it existed before the new law was passed.

Pay attention to what the conference agreement section says: that's where they tell you what was actually passed. It will usually say that the conference agreement follows the House (or Senate) provision, telling you which to read to see what the change was. Sometimes it will say it follows one or the other and then gives some modifications and occasionally it will have a whole new description telling you what the new law is. If it says: "The conference agreement does not contain the House (or Senate) bill provision." – it means the law was not changed. Sorry they use this stupid way to say nothing changed. The link goes to a government document, on a government website, so don't be pissed at me if they stop working.

UPDATE: As I've discovered the hard way, last minute wrangling caused some things to be changed AFTER the conference agreement was written. I think I have found and updated them all in the book, but be aware that the 1000-page document I linked was not the last word on the subject. One example was that the document includes language allowing the use of 529 college savings plan money for homeschool expenses, but this was removed at the last minute because it was not "fiscal" enough to be considered as part of a bill that can't be filibustered.

UPDATE: The IRS has a page dedicated to the tax law changes:

https://www.irs.gov/tax-reform

DISCLAIMER:
Because lawyers suck and people are greedy, it's important to point out that this book represents MY opinions and interpretations, and are not necessarily those of the IRS or my employer. These chapters are short and sweet, so they don't cover all details and may not be accurate for your situation. Do your own research to be certain. Talk to a competent professional. Do not rely solely on this book. Also, client confidentiality is important, so the spirit of client stories is true, but the details are significantly altered.

What Didn't Change

There was a lot of talk, and two passed bills, that went into the conference committee where the final bill language was decided.

Here's a list of things they talked about, but didn't change:

Capital Gains tax rates stayed the same
Identification of sold securities unchanged (no forced FIFO) *
No change to education credits
Student loan interest is still deductible
Savings bond interest used for education is still tax free
Colleges can still provide tax free education to their employees
Electric vehicle credit wasn't changed
Employer education expense exclusion is unchanged
No change to MSA deductibility
No change to educator expense deduction**
No change to the sale of personal residence exclusion***
No change to Dependent Care Benefits exclusion
No change to adoption rules
No change to the solar credit
No change to the Credit for Elderly and Disabled
No change to Mortgage Credit Certificates****
No change to Earned Income Credit
No change to employer provided housing rules
No change to exempt organizations rules on "politicking"
529 plans still can't be used for homeschool expenses

*There was a proposal to force partial sales of batches of stocks or other assets to be determined based on "First In, First Out" rules, rather than allowing the person selling to specify what shares of stock among a batch were the ones sold. This was not adopted.

**As will be discussed later, a whole bunch of itemized deductions were eliminated including the employee business expense deduction that teachers often use to deduct expenses above the $250 educator expense deduction.

***I am actually going to briefly cover the rules in a later chapter since people still think they have to buy a new home to make this work – something that was changed over 20 years ago.

****Links to my blog post on the subject for South Carolina

You Can Read the Law

Even better, there's an executive summary that tells you what the current law is, the Senate proposal, the House proposal, and what the final agreement was, mostly in English. I'm linking to it all here. The link will go to the summary page, skipping all the legalese. If you want to see how awful it is to read tax laws as they pass, scroll back a bit after clicking the link and see what it looks like. You will probably never want to see anything like that ever again, but it will give you an appreciation for what us tax dudes do when we try to figure it out.

http://docs.house.gov/billsthisweek/20171218/CRPT-115HRPT-466.pdf#page=524

For the most part, all changes affect 2018, so will impact the tax return you file in 2019. There's a lot of waffling as to when they will get withholding changed for 2018, so you might see most of the effect when you get your refund (or balance due). The IRS and payroll companies are saying that withholding will be changed by February, but I'm not absolutely counting on it.

UPDATE: Payroll withholding was changed for everyone by March and my gut level thought is that they slightly over-adjusted so refunds might go down slightly for most people, even if they're overall taxes go down. It's still a good idea to use the IRS withholding calculator discussed in later chapters to setup your withholding allowances for the refund or balance due that works for you.

I will specify the changes that don't happen in 2018, whether they are delayed or retroactively applied.

I am going to include links to the explanations of the law, as presented by the Congressional committee that negotiated the compromise bill. They may not work forever, since it's a government website. The sections start with the current law, then the House proposal, then the Senate proposal, and finally, what was agreed upon.

Here's another interesting link to the bill, where they discuss the complexity of the new law:

http://docs.house.gov/billsthisweek/20171218/CRPT-115HRPT-466.pdf#page=1078

The New Tax Rates

The new law makes most tax rates better for almost everyone. Generally speaking, a given amount of taxable income (after all deductions, but before credits) will have a lower amount of tax on it. There was a lot of talk of simplification, but we had 7 tax brackets before the new law passed, and we still have 7. Before they were 10 percent, 15, 25, 28, 33, 35 and 39.6. Now they are 10 percent, 12, 22, 24, 32, 35 and 37. The points at which you moved brackets changed as well.

Now, to settle a common misconception, when you cross into a bracket, you don't suddenly pay that rate on all your income, just the amount in the new bracket. As an example, a Single person, under the new rates, will ALWAYS pay 10 percent on their taxable income up to $9,525, and then 12 percent above that, up to the next bracket at $38,700. Only the portion of their taxable income above $38,700 gets taxed at 22% (up to the start of the next bracket.)

Here's a link to the new rates and brackets if you want to see them:

http://docs.house.gov/billsthisweek/20171218/CRPT-115HRPT-466.pdf#page=535

Most People Will Get a Tax Break

The law is almost universally positive for all but a very few taxpayers. This does not mean it's a good law (or a bad law) just that the vast majority of people will pay less taxes under the new regime. Most estimates peg the improvement at between 10 and 20 percent. So, if you paid $3000 in taxes in 2017, you will pay $300 to $600 less in 2018.

UPDATE: Use of my tax conversion calculator on the tax returns that I performed in 2018 (for 2017 tax year returns) resulted in only 24 of over 600 clients seeing higher taxes if the exact same return was calculated using the new law. While this is obviously anecdotal and subject to regional variations, it does bode well for most people.

This doesn't mean your refund will improve. The IRS will make adjustments to withholding tables, which should distribute these savings to you via your paycheck, with each check being slightly bigger. This "should" happen in by February, where you should see a little (or big) raise if you are like most people. People pay attention to their refund, but the effect of this bill will be in the amount of taxes that the IRS keeps before sending your refund, not the refund itself.

UPDATE: Based on very limited and anecdotal information, I am guessing many people's refunds will be slightly lower on their 2018 returns, even if their overall taxes went down. This assumes no major life changes and no adjustments made by the taxpayer to their withholding.

I have a chapter later that discusses what things might make you pay MORE taxes due to this bill, so you can be prepared if you're one of the unlucky ones.

Standard Deduction, Itemizing and Exemptions

To make the next few chapters clearer, I'm going to review a few things. Everyone is allowed to either take a "Standard" deduction, based on their filing status, or prove that they have more "Itemized" deductions than the standard one. Then they deduct the bigger number – either taking the Standard Deduction or Itemizing. There are some deductions that you get without itemizing, such as student loan interest, but we'll talk about those later. In addition to the standard deduction, you used to get an "exemption" for everyone you claimed as a dependent. This was $4050 in 2017.

Once you took all your deductions, you had "taxable income" and you figured the "tax" on this amount, usually using the tax tables, and sometimes special rates such as for capital gains. Then you got "credits". These credits directly reduce the tax amount. These are much better than deductions or exemptions. Most credits can't get your tax amount below zero, but some, "refundable" credits can actually reduce your tax below zero and get you back more money than you paid in!

For certain dependents, essentially children under the age of 17, you get a Child Tax Credit ($1000 before the new bill). Before the new law passed, all of it could be refundable for most people.

The next few chapters will go over the changes to the Standard Deduction, Exemptions, Child Tax Credit and Itemized Deductions.

The New Standard Deductions

The changes to the Standard Deduction will affect everyone, and they seem pretty amazing, but it's not all that it seems. Standard Deduction is based on filing status, which I'm not going to go into in detail. The Single (S) and Married Filing Separately (MFS) Standard Deduction went from $6,350 to $12,000. Head of Household (HH) went from $9,350 to $18,000. Married Filing Jointly (MFJ) and Qualifying Widower (QW) went from $12,700 to $24,000. This means a lot of people who used to itemize will be taking the standard deduction. This is one of the big reasons that this bill is spoken of as "simplifying" the tax code. The additions for being over 65 and blind were left unchanged.

Here's the catch: as we will see in the next section, they eliminated the $4050 exemption for EVERYONE. Since everyone filing a tax return gets an exemption (except people being claimed as dependents) this means S, QW, MFS and HH filers lost $4050 in exemptions, and MFJ lost $8100 in exemptions (one for the taxpayer and one for the spouse).

So, the actual effective change was:

Single went from $10,400 to $12,000
HH from $13,400 to $18,000
MFJ from $20,800 to $24,000.

HH looks pretty good, unless their dependent is 17 or over. In that case the loss of the Child Tax Credit effectively eliminates most of the benefit from the increase in Standard Deduction.

People with a LOT of itemized deductions are one of the categories of people might do worse under the new plan – and this section gives you an idea why.

If you think you will be above the 2017 standard deduction, but below the 2018 one, you can pay 2018 property taxes that have already been assessed, make your January mortgage payment in 2017, and get stuff to Goodwill or other charities in 2017.

UPDATE: The new standard deductions listed are for 2018. They will be adjusted for inflation going forward, so the will go up slightly every year. If you are close to the standard deduction, but still below it, grouping deductions you can manipulate (such as charity) into a single year, while taking the standard deduction in other years, is a way to maximize the effect of those deductions. I personally try to itemize every 3 years.

Read the Bill:

http://docs.house.gov/billsthisweek/20171218/CRPT-115HRPT-466.pdf#page=537

Exemptions Are Eliminated

As it was hinted last chapter, the $4050 exemption for dependents and taxpayers is GONE. For the filers (taxpayer and spouse) it was made up for in the standard deduction increase. For children, it was made up for in the Child Tax Credit increase (next chapter). For other dependents and children 17 and over, it is only partially made up for.

The only real thing to discuss here is that the entire W-4 process (how you tell your employer how much to take out of your paycheck for taxes) is based upon exemptions. The law allows the IRS to use exemptions on the W-4 through 2018, but we're not sure how they are going to account for this going forward, or even in the current year. Luckily, most people will see a tax improvement, so if they do nothing, you'll just get a bigger refund.

UPDATE: the IRS will continue to use allowances on the W-4, so the mechanics of it have not changed. The instructions have changed slightly to reflect the changes to the law. I still recommend using the withholding calculator on the IRS website rather than the instructions on the W-4.

Here's a link to the instruction page for the calculator:

https://www.irs.gov/individuals/irs-withholding-calculator

Read the Bill:

http://docs.house.gov/billsthisweek/20171218/CRPT-115HRPT-466.pdf#page=538

New Credits for Kids and Dependents

The Child Tax Credit, the one that you get for children under 17 (I'm not going to go into great detail on this since it's complicated, but if you got $1000 for them in 2017, and they didn't turn 17, this probably applies to them), has been increased from $1000 to $2000. Also, while in 2017 it could all be refundable, in 2018 and beyond only $1400 can be refundable. The rules calculating how much can be refundable are the same except the earned income floor was lowered from $3000 to $2500 (you take the amount of earned income you have (wages and self-employment income for the most part) subtract $2500 from it and multiply that by 15%. That is the maximum amount of the credit you can get after you have reduced your taxes to zero.)

UPDATE: Going forward, you can generally assume you will get the $2000 Child Tax Credit if you got it in the previous year, the living situation of children has not changed, the child in question has not turned 17, and your income stays below the threshold discussed below.

Dependents who don't qualify for the $2000 credit now get a $500 credit. Remember that credits come directly off taxes, not income. The $500 credit is non-refundable (can't reduce taxes below zero).

The rules for who qualifies as a dependent have not changed substantially.

Because of the elimination of exemptions just discussed, these improvements aren't as awesome as they look. For children under 17, you essentially break even if you are in the 25% tax bracket (discounting tax rate and bracket changes), do better in the 15% or below, and worse in the higher brackets. For other dependents, only those in the 10% or below brackets will see an improvement, all others will lose some money. Again, this is just taking the exemption and dependent credits into account in determining "break-even". Other aspects of the tax law change should help most people.

One HUGE change that will help some families is that the income limit above which the credit starts to disappear was raised to $200,000 ($400,000 for Married Filing Jointly). The old level for Married Filing Jointly was $110,000.

The child MUST have a valid Social Security Number to get the refundable portion of the Child Tax Credit.

Read the Bill:

http://docs.house.gov/billsthisweek/20171218/CRPT-115HRPT-466.pdf#page=564

Mortgage Interest Deduction

This is an Itemized Deduction.

There were minor tweaks to the ability to deduct interest paid on a home loan. First, the good news: This only applies to mortgages acquired in 2018 or later. If you are already deducting mortgage interest you can continue to deduct it as before.

For new mortgages, they lowered how big a mortgage you can deduct interest on. Previously, you could deduct mortgage interest on the first $1,000,000 of mortgage. They lowered this to $750,000. This seems like a big deal, but the MOST you can lose is a deduction on $250,000 of mortgage. If you pay 5% interest, that's $12,500 in deduction. In the old 25% tax bracket, that would be $3125 (this would be partially offset by the new lower tax rates). This is not a huge amount of money that is going to change the decision process on buying a home. Also, we will later discuss that they eliminated the income limit on itemized deductions, so people who can afford big, expensive houses, won't have to worry about that.

Obviously as home prices and interest rates rise, the math gets worse on the "lost" $250,000.

They also eliminated the ability to deduct home equity debt taken out after purchase, so you can't buy a car with home equity and deduct the interest. This was a terrible idea anyway, so I'm glad they got rid of it.

Read the Bill:

http://docs.house.gov/billsthisweek/20171218/CRPT-115HRPT-466.pdf#page=599

State and Local Income Taxes

This is an Itemized Deduction.

They didn't change what kind of state and local taxes you can deduct. Essentially, you can still deduct state and local property taxes and income taxes (or sales tax instead). They did however, limit the amount you can deduct as an itemized deduction to a total of $10,000 ($5,000 if Married Filing Separately). This does not apply to businesses or rental property claimed on Schedules C and E, or other business returns, just itemized deductions. This will hurt in states with high income or property taxes.

One strategy to look at is checking both state income taxes AND sales tax. If both result in going over $10,000, you are better off taking sales tax, since you have to add back as income a state tax refund if you deducted income taxes (this will almost certainly not be true since they will have to come up with a way to ensure you don't pay taxes on something you didn't deduct, but using sales tax skips this issue completely).

As far as pre-paying taxes in 2017 so they will be fully deductible: If your property taxes have already been assessed, go for it. Income taxes will be attributed to the year they are for, so pre-paying won't help.

UPDATE: They figured out this potential pre-paying loophole and closed it.

This does NOT impact deducting of taxes for business and rental property. It ONLY affects Itemized Deductions.

Read the Bill:

http://docs.house.gov/billsthisweek/20171218/CRPT-115HRPT-466.pdf#page=601

Casualty and Theft Losses

This is an Itemized Deduction.

The change to this was short and sweet, but it's a big deal. Casualty losses are now only deductible if the loss was attributable to a disaster declared by the President.

The only real advice related to this is to make sure you have home/car/renter's insurance that is solid and up to date. Which you already should have.

The below is NOT an itemized deduction:

For disasters that occurred in 2016 ONLY: If you suffered unreimbursed losses that are attributable to one of the disasters that occurred in 2016, you can deduct these losses from your tax return as long as the loss exceeded $500. You don't need to itemize to do this (it can come on top of the standard deduction). The normal limitations for casualty loss deductions do not apply.

Read the Bill:

http://docs.house.gov/billsthisweek/20171218/CRPT-115HRPT-466.pdf#page=604

Gambling Losses and Charity

These are Itemized Deductions.

These changes were minor in nature. You can deduct gambling losses up to the amount of your winnings. The law clarifies that expenses other than gambling losses associated with gambling are subject to the same limit.

The only charitable contribution changes most people will care about are: An increase in the percentage of your income you can deduct as charity (believe it or not you could only deduct half of your income as a charitable contribution, no matter how much you gave – the rest gets carried over to the next year). The law raised this to 60%. Be aware that some types of contributions, such as stock that has increased in value, are subject to stricter limits. The other change is that you can't deduct a contribution if you receive the right to buy sporting event tickets due to the donation.

Read the Bill:

http://docs.house.gov/billsthisweek/20171218/CRPT-115HRPT-466.pdf#page=605

Medical Expense Limit Change

This is an Itemized Deduction.

You can deduct medical expenses, but several years ago, there was a floor, equal to 7.5% of your Adjusted Gross Income, below which you couldn't deduct them. It made sense, in that you didn't want to have to keep receipts for every little thing, so the limit ensured you only deducted medical expenses if they really impacted your finances. The Affordable Care Act was phasing in a change to that limit, making it 10% for everyone except people near 65 years and older.

For 2017 and 2018, the limit was dropped back to 7.5%. Note that this is retroactive to the tax return you are about to file. For 2019 and beyond, the 10% threshold applies.

Read the Bill:

http://docs.house.gov/billsthisweek/20171218/CRPT-115HRPT-466.pdf#page=622

Miscellaneous Itemized Deductions

These are Itemized Deductions (in case the title didn't clue you in).

ALL the miscellaneous itemized deductions subject to the 2% floor have been repealed. These are, in rough descending order of significance (only including ones that aren't totally obscure):

Employee Business Expense (when you pay for things or drive for your job)
Depreciation of Computer Used to Invest
Fees to Collect Interest and Dividends
Hobby Expenses
Investment Fees and expenses
Loss on IRA's after all Funds are Distributed
Safe Deposit Box Fees
Service Charges on Dividend Reinvestment Plans
Tax Preparation Fees and Expenses
Union Dues*
Educator Expenses (except the $250 non-itemized deduction) *
Boomer Deduction*
Rural Mail Carriers Vehicle Expense*
Employee Travel Expense*
Work Clothes and Uniforms*
Work Related Education*
Repayments of Social Security Benefits
Research Expense of College Professor

*These are all Employee Business Expenses, but I thought I'd state them separately for clarity. Some of these will be discussed in more detail later as they apply to specific situations.

It's important to understand that some of these mirror business expenses of business owners as opposed to employees. They have only been eliminated for employees. If you own a business, most of these are still deductible on your business return. There is a lot more information on businesses available further into the book.

Read the Bill:

http://docs.house.gov/billsthisweek/20171218/CRPT-115HRPT-466.pdf#page=618

Corporate Tax Rate

The tax rate for corporations was reduced to 21 percent. This and the 20 percent business taxable income deduction discussed in the next chapter, were intended to make having a business in the United States more attractive.

They are also intended to make corporate and other business tax rates closer to each other.

That's about all I'm going to say on the subject, because I'm guessing corporations have experts they're using to do their taxes, as opposed to this book.

There are major changes to how foreign income is taxed that are designed to bring businesses and income back to the U.S. I am NOT going into those, so this chapter is pretty fricken' short.

20% Business Deduction

The next three paragraphs will cover the changes for the vast majority of people. The rest is for people making a lot of money (relatively speaking).

This has been called the "pass-through" deduction, but that's not really accurate. It includes almost all business income, including sole-proprietorships, S corporations, limited liability companies and income from investments in publicly traded partnerships and real estate investment trusts. There's also a possibility that it applies to residential rental property (we're not sure about this yet – and may not know until mid-2018).

UPDATE: As far as rental property is concerned, it will be a "facts and circumstances" determination. If it's a business, based on "facts and circumstances" then it will be eligible for the deduction. Obviously, someone renting a former house out using a property manager probably won't qualify, but the more time spent on rentals, and the more businesslike it is run, the more likely it is to be eligible. Since most rentals start out at a loss, and these losses must be accounted for before eligible for the deduction, it seems most small landlords will find it more trouble than it's worth. That said, a decision needs to be made early how to try to handle this (though it can change as circumstances do) and professional help is probably warranted when deciding. This is a BIG complicated situation, with long-term implications, so paying for help early can be worth its weight in gold (or fees).

There are a lot of weird provisions that kick in above a certain income, but if your TAXABLE* income (income after virtually all deductions other than this one) is less than $157,500 ($315,000 Married Filing Jointly (MFJ)), then this pretty much applies to all business income and you get to deduct 20% of your net profit from each business directly off of your taxable income. This is designed to cause all businesses to pay about the same tax rate as corporations do with the new lower corporate rate.

Above those numbers, a lot of weirdness kicks in.

If your business is service oriented** and your taxable income is over $157,500 ($315,000 MFJ), then your deduction starts to phase out and will be completely gone at $207,500 ($415,000 MFJ).

If your taxable income is $157,500 ($315,000 MFJ) and you have a non-service business, then the deduction is up to 20% of business income, but subject to a limitation based on wages or depreciable property in service that also phases in such that the limit fully applies at taxable income of $207,500 ($415,000 MFJ).

The wage limitation when fully phased in applies such that the most you can deduct is the greater of 50% of W-2 wages paid by the company (including your own wages) or 25% of W-2 wages plus 2.5% of the original basis of all qualified property***

This is both an over-simplified explanation and an explanation based on VERY early readings of a VERY complicated change. While I have discussed this with a lot of very smart tax people, it is likely that we might be missing or misinterpreting some aspects of this change. If there's a chance this applies to you beyond very small dollar amounts, suck it up and pay a really good professional for help this year.

UPDATE: A lot more has become clear, but I still stand by the suggestion of professional help, especially if you have multiple businesses or are above the income thresholds.

*This rule is very unusual in that you have to do your tax return all the way through just before figuring your tax, and THEN apply this deduction. It uses taxable income for virtually all tests and calculations, as opposed to Gross or Adjusted Gross Income like almost everything else in the tax world.

**From the bill, "A specified service trade or business means any trade or business involving the performance of services in the fields of health, law, consulting, athletics, financial services, brokerage services, or any trade or business where the principal asset of such trade or business is the reputation or skill of one or more of its employees or owners, or which involves the performance of services that consist of investing and investment management trading, or dealing in securities, partnership interests, or commodities." Architects and engineers are specifically noted as NOT subject to this limitation.

***From the Bill: "qualified property means tangible property of a character subject to depreciation that is held by, and available for use in, the qualified trade or business at the close of the taxable year, and which is used in the production of qualified business income, and for which the depreciable period has not ended before the close of the taxable year. The depreciable period with respect to qualified property of a taxpayer means the period beginning on the date the property is first placed in service by the taxpayer and ending on the later of (a) the date 10 years after that date, or (b) the last day of the last full year in the applicable recovery period that would apply to the property under section 168 (without regard to section 168(g))."

Read the Bill:

http://docs.house.gov/billsthisweek/20171218/CRPT-115HRPT-466.pdf#page=543

How Does This Affect My Business?

Lots of changes, the biggest of which is the new 20% deduction for "pass-through" entities, that definitely applies to sole proprietorships, partnerships and S corporations. There's a whole previous chapter on that, so I'm not going to rehash it here. Same with the reduction of the corporate tax rate to 21%.

The limit on deductions for state and local taxes doesn't apply to businesses. There has been no change to the deductibility of state and local taxes by businesses.

They extended bonus depreciation for another few years, through 2026 (click the link for a breakdown of how it decreases.) They also expanded the amount of section 179 deduction you can take in a year to $1,000,000 and expanded what items qualify. Both changes will allow you to deduct more money from capital expenditures in the year you make them.

http://docs.house.gov/billsthisweek/20171218/CRPT-115HRPT-466.pdf#page=702
http://docs.house.gov/billsthisweek/20171218/CRPT-115HRPT-466.pdf#page=735

More businesses qualify to use the cash method of accounting:

http://docs.house.gov/billsthisweek/20171218/CRPT-115HRPT-466.pdf#page=738

They eliminated the ability to carryback Net Operating Losses, they must now be carried forward to future years:

http://docs.house.gov/billsthisweek/20171218/CRPT-115HRPT-466.pdf#page=757

Almost all entertainment expenses, other than meals for employees (or facilities for them) have been made non-deductible:

http://docs.house.gov/billsthisweek/20171218/CRPT-115HRPT-466.pdf#page=769

There are a lot more obscure changes that most people wouldn't understand and that are pretty complicated, especially involving foreign investment and income. I'm not going to bury you with those here.

Inflation Adjustment Changes

There are many provisions of tax law that are "inflation adjusted". This basically means that they go up as the cost of living goes up. The new law changes how this is calculated, in a way that is not favorable to taxpayers, but is minor initially (though the effect will be magnified as it is compounded over years). They used to use the Consumer Price Index, but now will use something called the Chained Consumer Price Index.

Explanations for this are way too wonky to include here, except to mention that it means tax benefits will be muted going forward, due to things like tax brackets and deductions going up more slowly over time than they would otherwise.

Read the Bill:

http://docs.house.gov/billsthisweek/20171218/CRPT-115HRPT-466.pdf#page=540

2016 Presidential Disasters

No, we're not talking about politics or President Trump! We're specifically talking about events that were declared disasters by the President in accordance with the Robert T. Stafford Disaster Relief and Emergency Assistance Act (The Stafford Act). Also, only those that occurred in 2016. There are two major types of relief. The ability to use money from your retirement account without penalty, and a deduction for your unreimbursed losses.

You can find a summary of all disasters using the link at this website. It downloads an Excel spreadsheet that has every disaster, EVER, so you need to scroll down to find the 2016 ones:

https://www.fema.gov/media-library/assets/documents/28318

Retirement Account Provisions:

If you lived in the area of a Presidential declared disaster area in 2016 (principal place of abode), you can take money out of your 401k or other employer retirement account to cover for your losses (losses have to occur in 2016 or 2017 for a disaster that occurred in 2016). You can do this without paying the 10% penalty on early withdrawals, AND, you can pay taxes on it over three years OR, you can put it back in within 3 years and pay NO taxes on it.

Here's the text from the conference agreement explaining it:

"A qualified 2016 disaster distribution is a distribution from an eligible retirement plan made on or after January 1, 2016, and before January 1, 2018, to an individual whose principal place of abode at any time during calendar year 2016 was located in a 2016 disaster area and who has sustained an economic loss by reason of the events giving rise to the Presidential disaster declaration. The total amount of distributions to an individual from all eligible retirement plans that may be treated as qualified 2016 disaster distributions is $100,000. Thus, any distributions in excess of $100,000 during the applicable period are not qualified 2016 disaster distributions.

Any amount required to be included in income as a result of a qualified 2016 disaster is included in income ratably over the three-year period beginning with the year of distribution unless the individual elects not to have ratable inclusion apply.

Any portion of a qualified 2016 disaster distribution may, at any time during the three-year period beginning the day after the date on which the distribution was received, be recontributed to an eligible retirement plan to which a rollover can be made. Any amount recontributed within the three-year period is treated as a rollover and thus is not includible in income.

For example, if an individual receives a qualified 2016 disaster distribution in 2016, that amount is included in income, generally ratably over the year of the distribution and the following two years, but is not subject to the 10-percent early withdrawal tax. If, in 2018, the amount of the qualified 2016 disaster distribution is recontributed to an eligible retirement plan, the individual may file an amended return to claim a refund of the tax attributable to the amount previously included in income. In addition, if, under the ratable inclusion provision, a portion of the distribution has not yet been included in income at the time of the contribution, the remaining amount is not includible in income."

If you took money out in 2016, you can go back and modify your tax returns to take advantage of this.

Disaster Loss Deduction:

If you suffered unreimbursed losses that are attributable to one of the disasters that occurred in 2016, you can deduct these losses from your tax return as long as the loss exceeded $500. You don't need to itemize to do this (it can come on top of the standard deduction). The normal limitations for casualty loss deductions (which were eliminated with this bill anyway) do not apply. *

*You used to have to deduct $100 per event and only deduct the part above 10% of your income AND it was an itemized deduction.

Read the Bill:

http://docs.house.gov/billsthisweek/20171218/CRPT-115HRPT-466.pdf#page=686

Sunset Provisions

Many of these changes expire in 2025. I'm not even going to talk about what ones they apply to and when they sunset (though partisan talking heads are calling it a future tax increase) because we all know that Congress will change everything by then and, even if they don't, they won't just let them expire – too much political pressure.

This means that I may say something has been eliminated, even though it actually has been "suspended". I simply can't be bothered to play the silly political games that were required to keep the bill under $1.5 trillion dollars of cost.

So, we'll worry about it in 2023 or later.

States That Start with Taxable Income

One of the under-appreciated aspects of this bill is how it will affect the few states that start their tax calculation with Federal Taxable Income.

Most states start with Adjusted Gross Income, which is calculated BEFORE standard/itemized deductions and exemptions. Some start with Gross Income, which is before EVERY deduction, some use their own system entirely, and a very few start with Taxable Income.

Most states will see some effect transferred from the Federal changes to their return, but the changes to the standard deductions and exemptions mean these will be exaggerated in states that start with Taxable Income. If you live in one of these states, watch for law changes to account for this, or expect your state tax return to improve or degrade along with the Federal.

States that (as best I could tell at time of publishing) start with Taxable Income are:

Colorado
Minnesota
North Dakota
South Carolina
Vermont (updated below)

UPDATE: Many states have been tweaking their laws to account for expected effects on their tax receipts. These are too numerous to discuss here, except to note that Vermont has decoupled from taxable income and that most tax schemes by high tax states to turn their taxes into charitable deductions to evade the State Tax deduction limit were squashed by the IRS.

Working from Home or Tele-Commuting

If you didn't already figure it out, you're getting hosed. The elimination of the employee business expenses essentially prevents you from deducting any of the costs of working from home.

The 2% floor prevented a lot of people from taking advantage of this, and the increase in the standard deduction will take some of the sting out of it, but for some people this might really hurt.

You are going to have to decide if working from home is still worth it, or if you can negotiate an increase in salary from your employer. Keep in mind that the salary increase will probably all be taxable, but more money is more money. You can also consider trying to get your employer to pay for some of the things that you would normally pay for when working from home.

Your tax dude should be able to give you an idea as to what kind of hit you are going to take when you file your 2017 taxes. Use this when you negotiate. If negotiations don't work, look for a new job (but be aware that moving and job-hunting expenses are no longer deductible either.)

UPDATE: Once you file your 2018 tax return, you should have a much better idea how this affected you and have additional ammunition for negotiations with your employer. Make sure you discuss this with your tax professional or take a careful look at your return if you prepare it yourself.

Driving and Travelling for Work (esp Sales)

This chapter is basically the same as the last chapter, except to emphasize that mileage was probably a HUGE deduction for you, and negotiations discussed below (in the cut and paste from the previous chapter) should include talk of a company car or mileage reimbursement. If you are a kick ass salesman, you should be able to make this work.

Truckers paid on a W-2 are going to be hard hit in this area, so be prepared to talk to your employer.

Begin cut and paste section:

If you didn't already figure it out, you're getting hosed. The elimination of the employee business expenses essentially prevents you from deducting any of the costs of working from home.

The 2% floor prevented a lot of people from taking advantage of this, and the increase in the standard deduction will take some of the sting out of it, but for some people this might really hurt.

You are going to have to decide if working from home is still worth it, or if you can negotiate an increase in salary from your employer. Keep in mind that the salary increase will probably all be taxable, but more money is more money. You can also consider trying to get your employer to pay for some of the things that you would normally pay for when working from home.

Your tax dude should be able to give you an idea as to what kind of hit you are going to take when you file your 2017 taxes. Use this when you negotiate. If negotiations don't work, look for a new job (but be aware that moving and job-hunting expenses are no longer deductible either.)

UPDATE: Once you file your 2018 tax return, you should have a much better idea how this affected you and have additional ammunition for negotiations with your employer. Make sure you discuss this with your tax professional or take a careful look at your return if you prepare it yourself.

What Should I Be Doing Now?

Pay attention to your withholding. You should see the effect of the new tax law in your paycheck starting in February. If that change goes in the wrong direction based on what this book has lead you to expect, get it adjusted. Hopefully the IRS will update their withholding calculator, and you can use that to figure out what should be on your W-4:

https://www.irs.gov/individuals/irs-withholding-calculator

Talk to your tax person to see what you can expect. I have created a calculator that you can use to convert 2017 tax information into 2018 results, so check it out. That said, nothing is a substitute for good tax advice. For you software users, I'm just going to say that I'm adding this tax law change as a reason I hate software (chapter later). Make sure you aren't going to owe. If you are unsure, an emergency fund (also discussed in this book) is a great idea in case you (or your tax dude) mess this up.

If you are losing a big deduction that is job related, negotiate with your employer to see if they will pick up the slack. How well you can do this depends on how indispensable you are to your employer. It's always a good idea to be irreplaceable!

Get a Social Security Number for your child if you don't already have one.

If you think you will be above the 2017 standard deduction, but below the 2018, you can pay 2018 property taxes that have already been assessed, make your January mortgage payment in 2017, and get stuff to Goodwill or other charities in 2017. Get hot, not a lot of days left (if any – I don't know when you bought the book).

Relax. Taxes are way down on the list of things to sweat. For most people, this will be a non-event that they don't even notice as the benefits (or pain) are spread out over 20 plus paychecks.

Here's a link to the place where I put the calculator, as well as some other worksheets:

http://supertaxgenius.blogspot.com/2017/12/book-owner-exclusives.html

How Do I Know I'm Not One of the Few Getting Hosed?

Here are some situations where you might be one of the few who don't do well under this new law:

1. You live in a state with very high state income taxes and/or property taxes. If you pay significantly more than $10,000 in these taxes, you could be in trouble, especially if your itemized deductions were much bigger than the standard deduction.

UPDATE: Many high tax states are getting creative trying to circumvent the $10,000 limitation. Don't get your hopes up. The IRS has squashed the majority of them, though some states are suing over this.

2. You tele-commute or deduct a lot of mileage as an employee. There are chapters on this, with advice.

3. You deducted anything that could be considered entertainment.

4. You file Married Filing Separately. The IRS hates this filing status, and the punishment has only gotten worse.

5. You had a not for profit rental or hobby with significant deductions on Schedule A.

6. Unrelated to the tax bill, but sometimes life changes can hurt your taxes. Getting married, kids turning 17, and major income increases can all mess up your taxes. Even if you are getting benefits from the tax bill, these life changes can turn it in the other direction. Especially kids turning 17!

Is my Rental Property Affected?

Maybe. But probably not. If it is, probably in a good way.

The change in deductibility of mortgage interest and real estate taxes does not affect your rental property. Changes in depreciation rules also make very little difference here.

It looks like the new 20% deduction for business income MIGHT apply to you, but we're honestly not sure. That, plus the fact that most rentals operate at a taxable loss, means that you will probably see zero effect on your rental property with regard to taxes.

UPDATE: As far as rental property is concerned, it will be a "facts and circumstances" determination. If it's a business, based on "facts and circumstances" then it will be eligible for the deduction. Obviously, someone renting a former house out using a property manager probably won't qualify, but the more time spent on rentals, and the more businesslike it is run, the more likely it is to be eligible. Since most rentals start out at a loss, and these losses must be accounted for before eligible for the deduction, it seems most small landlords will find it more trouble than it's worth. That said, a decision needs to be made early how to try to handle this (though it can change as circumstances do) and professional help is probably warranted when deciding. This is a BIG complicated situation, with long-term implications, so paying for help early can be worth its weight in gold (or fees).

If you have a not for profit rental, where you were deducting expenses on Schedule A instead of Schedule E, you can no longer deduct expenses, but you still have to claim the income.

Alimony

In the past, alimony paid was deducted by the person paying it, and included as income by the person receiving it. This has been eliminated starting in 2019.

Affecting 2019 and later: Obviously Congress recognized that people were actively negotiating divorces that would take effect in 2018, so they delayed this part of the law until 2019. This only applies to NEW divorce agreements. If you are already paying alimony, nothing has changed. Starting with 2019 settlements, the payment of alimony is a tax neutral event (nobody deducts it and nobody includes it as income).

If you end up negotiating a divorce that will be signed in 2019, make sure you take these changes into account.

Read the Bill:

http://docs.house.gov/billsthisweek/20171218/CRPT-115HRPT-466.pdf#page=623

Moving Expenses No Longer Deductible

If you moved for work, you used to be able to deduct a lot of things you had to pay for the move. If your employer paid them, you didn't have to pay taxes on that money. Now you can't deduct ANYTHING for moving. If your employer reimburses you, or pays moving expenses for you, you have to pay taxes on that money as if they paid it for work. (This is over-simplified, so talk to a professional or your Human Resources if you have moving expenses paid or reimbursed by your employer).

Many companies used to pay you extra to cover taxes on reimbursements that weren't deductible or excludable (like house buying assistance). Employees should be looking to negotiate these extra payments for entire moves if they have leverage.

This change does not apply to active duty military moving on Permanent Change of Station Orders.

Read the Bill:

http://docs.house.gov/billsthisweek/20171218/CRPT-115HRPT-466.pdf#page=624
http://docs.house.gov/billsthisweek/20171218/CRPT-115HRPT-466.pdf#page=633

Estate Taxes

The exemption was effectively doubled, but in a weird way. It was made $10,000,000, but indexed for inflation from back in 2010, so the exemption calculates out to $11.200,000 in 2018, and will go up from there until it reverts back to $5,000,000 on January 1st, 2026 (unless action is taken.)

This means that the estate of someone who dies in 2018 can exclude $11,200,000 from estate taxes. That number goes up for every year after 2018 until 2026, when it drops back down.

Read the Bill:

http://docs.house.gov/billsthisweek/20171218/CRPT-115HRPT-466.pdf#page=657

Changes to the Alternative Minimum Tax

Alternative Minimum Tax (AMT) is complicated. It is essentially a separate tax system, where they take away most deductions, and replace them with one big exemption, and apply a nearly flat tax rate. The exemption is reduced if you make too much money.

The new tax law dramatically raises the exemption from $84,500 Married Filing Joint (MFJ), $54,300 Single (S) or Head of Household (HH) and $42,250 Married Filing Separately (MFS) to $109,400 MFJ, $70,300 S or HH and $54,700 MFS. These are some pretty nice new numbers.

They also raise the point at which the exemption starts dropping to $1,000,000 MFJ and $500,000 for all other filing statuses. For perspective, the old value was $160,900 for MFJ. This is also a big deal.

This means a lot fewer people are going to be subject to the AMT, and, if you are like most people flirting with it, you will be able to relax for a while.

The way the AMT is implemented on a tax return is to calculate both regular and AMT tax and, if AMT is higher, the difference is added to the regular tax amount. State and local taxes (SALT), medical expenses and exemptions are some common things that the AMT limits or eliminates. Anyone who has done a tax return that has entered AMT range has seen how adding taxes or exemptions makes no more difference. Many changes to the tax laws, like the limitation to SALT, more medical expense deductibility, exemption elimination and new tax tables have the effect of moving you closer or further away from AMT, depending on their effect. This means predicting the effect on a specific tax return is going to be very hard, as will tax planning for AMT. All we can really say is that AMT is going to affect a lot fewer people – hopefully you're not one of the ones who get hit.

Read the Bill:

http://docs.house.gov/billsthisweek/20171218/CRPT-115HRPT-466.pdf#page=668

The Penalty for Not Having Insurance is Gone (soon)

This has been eliminated. Starting in 2019 the shared responsibility payment, and all its exceptions have been eliminated, but not until 2019 – so you still need insurance in 2018. There is no sunset provision, making the change permanent.

To be clear, we are talking about the Affordable Care Act's penalty, of up to 2.5% of your income that is imposed for not having health insurance.

Read the Bill:

http://docs.house.gov/billsthisweek/20171218/CRPT-115HRPT-466.pdf#page=676

The Kiddie Tax is Easier Now

The "Kiddie Tax" was one of the most irritating aspects of tax law before this new tax bill. It was designed to prevent parents from transferring investments to their kids to avoid paying a fair rate of taxes on it. The way they did this was annoying, complicated and stupid. Essentially, if your child had more than $2100 of investment income (though they included all unearned income, even unemployment) the taxes were paid at the rate it would have been had it been on the parent's tax return. Needless to say, this was a mess. Parents could also include it on their return as if it was their income.

The kiddie tax applied to kids until they turned 18, or up to 24 if they didn't provide over half their own support. This has not been changed.

The new law basically eliminates the kiddie tax, and taxes investment income of children as if it was in a trust/estate. This taxes it at a higher rate than if it was just the kid's income, but not at a variable rate based on their parents. I'm not sure how they are going to implement this, but it can probably be handled directly on the child's tax return, with maybe one additional form.

UPDATE: Form 8615 will be used to calculate the taxes on the child's return. The tax rates go as high as 37%. Below is a link to the 2018 Form Instructions, which has the tax rates on the first page:

https://www.irs.gov/pub/irs-pdf/i8615.pdf

Head of Household Issues

Most people will probably not notice what they did with Head of Household on this bill, but it actually matters. They didn't change the numbers or requirements. What they did, is make it more important not to cheat in this area.

Some background (my personal interpretation of motivations is included and could be wrong): A couple years ago, Congress figured out (or finally acknowledged) how much fraud there was involved in refundable credits like the Earned Income Credit, Additional Child Tax Credit and the American Opportunity Credit. To combat this, they tightened the rules on documentation and reporting, AND they added a due diligence requirement on tax professionals. For all intents and purposes, I'm allowed to believe my clients when they tell me something, even if it seems weird or far-fetched. For those credits I just mentioned, they changed that and require me to ask and document additional questions if information provided doesn't add up or seems inconsistent. I also have to inform my clients of the importance of being honest and the repercussions of failing to be.

This should give you the idea that they are paying close attention to these areas, and the number of letters I've seen regarding the American Opportunity Credit in particular bear this out.

The new law extends these requirements to claiming Head of Household starting in 2019. So make sure you know the rules and follow them.

What About Your Withholding

The entire system upon which withholding is based uses your marital status and a number of exemptions reported by you on a W-4 form. The exemptions on the W-4 roughly equate to the number of people claimed on a tax return, but in practice it never worked very well. The elimination of exemptions has thrown this for a loop. The law allows the IRS to continue using number of exemptions to determine withholding through the end of 2018. After that, we have no idea how they plan on calculating withholding amounts.

You should not need to adjust your withholding to account for the changes in tax brackets, exemptions, standard deduction or itemized deductions. Withholding tables SHOULD be adjusted by February and the modification will appear in your paycheck.

If other aspects of the bill affect you, you should either talk to a professional, or use the IRS withholding calculator to determine how to adjust your withholding. I would wait until April before doing this, just to give them time to update the calculator for the new law. This will put you a little behind the eight ball, but the calculator takes accumulated withholding into account, so it will work out for 2018. The thing to make certain of, however, is that you go BACK to the calculator in January of 2019, to adjust the numbers for a full year.

UPDATE: the IRS will continue to use allowances on the W-4, so the mechanics of it have not changed. The instructions have changed slightly to reflect the changes to the law. I still recommend using the withholding calculator on the IRS website rather than the instructions on the W-4.

https://www.irs.gov/individuals/irs-withholding-calculator

The IRS is NOT Ready for This Law

The IRS is currently understaffed and underfunded, at least according to them and some other news outlets. This law is not going to help. It has been passed when the IRS is gearing up for the 2017 tax season, and does not provide significant resources for them to do all the new things they need to do.

Right away they have to update withholding tables for businesses to know how much to take out of your paycheck. In addition, they are likely to be flooded with calls asking about the affect of this, especially since enormous swaths of people seem to think it affects the tax return they are about to file (it doesn't).

The IRS needs to read the law, work with Congress to interpret the law, write regulations about the law, ask Congress to modify it when they discover the inevitable errors, then allow the regulations to be reviewed and commented upon before finalizing them.

Only after that can they start working on the publications that you use, and the forms and instructions.

Tax professionals are guessing as to exactly how the regulations are going to be written and exactly what some of the words that are ambiguous mean.

Tax software companies are going to have to jump through hoops to get ready for the 2019 filing season.

But here's the deal. You've got this book. You know the law doesn't affect the tax return you're about to file. You can expect withholding to be mostly handled.

Relax. Pay attention to your withholding and talk to a tax professional if you think something big in here is going to affect you. You have time.

UPDATE: Obviously, the IRS has published regulations and has most forms ready for the 2019 tax season. There will still be growing pains, but we have a lot better idea how things are supposed to work and will have an even better idea after the 2018 filing season (early 2019). There will still be litigation that can take many years, so it will be a while before every little detail is worked out.

Some Cancelled Student Loans Are Not Taxable

To be honest, this isn't so much a change as a clarification of where things were probably headed anyway.

A lot of people don't realize that when someone cancels debt that you owe, you often have to pay taxes on the cancelled debt as income. This is true of student loans. There are ways around it, mostly you use the insolvency exclusion to avoid claiming cancelled student loans as income.

The law made clear that if your loan is cancelled due to death or permanent and total disability, that the cancelled debt does not count as income. The IRS defines total and permanent disability different than you or I, but since you have to prove it to the student loan people to get your debt cancelled, proving it to the IRS will be easy.

I suspect that once this gets fully implemented, the student loan people won't even be reporting the cancelled loans to the IRS if you meet the requirements.

Read the Bill:

http://docs.house.gov/billsthisweek/20171218/CRPT-115HRPT-466.pdf#page=589

Not Good if Your Employer Pays You to Bike to Work

The old law allowed an employer to pay you up to $20 a month to defray the costs of you biking to work. They did not have to include this in income. This exclusion has been eliminated.

To be honest, the amount of money involved made this a symbolic exclusion only, so eliminating it might be the purist example of tax law "simplification" in the entire bill.

Read the Bill:

http://docs.house.gov/billsthisweek/20171218/CRPT-115HRPT-466.pdf#page=629

Calculating What YOUR Taxes Will Do

I have made a spreadsheet which will allow you to input your 2017 tax numbers and convert them to 2018. I have posted the link here:

http://supertaxgenius.blogspot.com/2017/12/book-owner-exclusives.html

Here are some calculators you can use right now (I cannot vouch for the accuracy of any of them):

http://www.cnn.com/2017/12/13/politics/calculate-americans-taxes-senate-reform-bill/index.html

https://www.nytimes.com/interactive/2017/12/17/upshot/tax-calculator.html

https://www.marketwatch.com/story/the-new-trump-tax-calculator-what-do-you-owe-2017-10-26

http://www.foxbusiness.com/politics/2017/12/19/tax-calculator-what-tax-reform-means-for.html

If You Have a Hobby That Makes Money

You're getting screwed.

A lot of people don't realize, that you have to report any income that you make, even if it's from a hobby or enterprise that you're not trying to make a profit on. Before the law change, you were allowed to deduct your expenses, but only up to the amount of income you made. You still didn't get that great of a deal, because you deducted them as an itemized deduction subject to the 2% of income limitations, which meant you both had to have enough deductions to make itemizing worth it, AND, even if you had enough to itemize, the 2% floor meant you didn't get all the benefit from your deductions.

As if that wasn't bad enough, making you claim all your income but not giving deductions the same treatment, now you can't deduct ANY hobby expenses. The entire 2% of income category of deductions was eliminated.

The only positive side is that the vast majority of hobbies don't make that much income, and the old limits to deductions means the change is unlikely to have a dramatic effect on most people's bottom line. But it's still BS.

College Savings Plans and Elementary and Secondary School

This section is about state-run 529 college savings plans. They have different names in different states, but, basically, they allow people to put money into tax deferred accounts for a designated person, for their later use to pay college expenses. If you take the money out for qualified college expenses, you don't pay taxes on the withdrawal.

The new law allows you to withdraw up to $10,000 per year, per student to pay for tuition related expenses at public, private or religious elementary and secondary (middle and high school) educational institutions.

A lot of states allow you to get a deduction for contributing to these accounts (almost always the one setup by your state of residence) and many have no limitation on the timing of withdrawals. This means that it's possible to contribute money that you've already earmarked for these kind of expenses, get a state tax deduction, and then pull it out and spend it as planned. I would suggest getting professional advice before doing this.

http://docs.house.gov/billsthisweek/20171218/CRPT-115HRPT-466.pdf#page=583

Entertainment Deduction Changes

Essentially all deductions for entertainment expenses have been eliminated. This applies to both businesses and employees (all employee business expense deductions were eliminated with the rest of the deductions subject to the 2% of Adjusted Gross Income limit). All expenses for any activity generally considered to be entertainment, amusement or recreation, as well as membership dues to any club organized for business, pleasure, recreation or other social purposes are now not deductible. Entertainment facilities are also not deductible.

The only expense that sort of fell in this category that survived, was the deduction for 50% of meals provided for employees or food and beverage expenses paid in conjunction with operating their business.

UPDATE: Meals where the taxpayer is present and that are not extravagant are still 50% deductible for current or potential business clients, customers, consultants or other business contacts.

Read the Bill:

http://docs.house.gov/billsthisweek/20171218/CRPT-115HRPT-466.pdf#page=769

Sexual Harassment Settlements

Companies will no longer be able to deduct payments they make in settlements to victims of alleged sexual harassment as a business expense. This applies to attorney's fees, settlements and other payments, but only if they are subject to a non-disclosure agreement.

It will be interesting to see how this affects sexual harassment suits and settlements. Will they just suck up the taxes? Will they pay without non-disclosure agreements? Or will they go to court more often? Hopefully this doesn't have the wrong impact, and actually makes people behave better.

Read the Bill:

http://docs.house.gov/billsthisweek/20171218/CRPT-115HRPT-466.pdf#page=802

Non-Profit Employees are Getting a Pay Cut

Maybe.

Pay to non-profit employees above one million dollars will now be subject to a 21% excise tax – but only for the 5 highest paid employees. The tax is paid by the company and not the executives. Not sure if non-profits will eat this, or if they are going to cut pay.

For perspective, in 2014, 2700 people were paid more than $1,000,000, mostly at hospitals. This is according to the Wall Street Journal.

What I'm interested in is how this will affect football coaches at some non-profit colleges. Yes, we're talking about people like Nick Saban.

Read the Bill:

http://docs.house.gov/billsthisweek/20171218/CRPT-115HRPT-466.pdf#page=869

Don't Believe What You Hear About the New Law

Unless you hear about it from a competent professional that you trust, it's very likely to be crap information. Government websites are usually reliable. Big financial publications (Kiplinger's for example) are pretty good. Newspapers and broadcast news are terrible. Blogs (other than mine), Facebook posts, friends, neighbors...all useless. Competent tax professionals are the only people you should trust for sure. You can't even trust IRS employees. Believe it or not, if you get an answer from the IRS over the phone, and it's wrong, it's still on you. You need it in writing. I wrote myself a note to list all the stupid things about taxes I've heard, but there's just no room, and no way to pick a winner.

Some Things to Know About How This Will be Implemented

What is passed is the LAW. Modifications to the Code of Federal Regulations 26 - IRS Code (though the law is written like an edit to the code - insert here, replace here, etc.)

The IRS will need to interpret it, and then issue proposed new REGULATIONS, which will be commented on, modified, and finally approved.

The Code and Regulations are the rules that must be followed. This will take until late in 2018.

Then they will update their PUBLICATIONS, FORMS and INSTRUCTIONS - that's how most people figure out what to do on their return, and part of how tax software is written. This might happen as late as January 2019 for some things.

Then people will do things on their taxes that the IRS doesn't like, and think violates the law. Some will go to court, and rulings will be made. The IRS will win some, and lose some. Once something is litigated we will finally have confidence what it means. This can take YEARS.

Bottom line, for many areas of the law, we won't have a true idea how they will be implemented and interpreted for quite some time (other areas are obvious).

UPDATE: Most regulations have been written and approved and forms and publications are being issued and most should be ready around the time they are needed for the 2018 tax filing season (early 2019).

Selling Your Home

As promised, I'm going to briefly discuss the rules for not having to pay taxes on any profit when you sell your home.

Before that, I'm going to remind you that if you LOSE money selling your home, you don't get to deduct the loss, which makes being able to exclude the gain seem fair.

So, if you owned AND lived in the home for 2 of the last 5 years, never rented it out and never ran a business out of the home, you can exclude up to $250,000 of profit on the sale of your home ($500,000 if filing Married Filing Jointly (MFJ)). You DO NOT have to reinvest the money in a new home. VERY basically, if the selling price minus what you paid for it is less than $250,000 ($500,000 MFJ) then you pay no taxes on the sale. Generally, at closing, one of the papers you sign will attest that you meet this exclusion, and they won't even report the sale to the IRS!

If you don't meet the times, but had to move for an unexpected reason, you might be able to get a portion of the exclusion. See a professional. If you used it for business or rented it out, see a professional.

Old Chapters:

The following pages include chapters from The Short Cheap Tax Book for Everyone that have been annotated or modified to fit the discussion of the tax law changes. A couple are included just because I want them in every book, because they are just that important.

Some of the advice is going to seem obvious, but 20 years doing taxes tells me that just because it's obvious to some people, doesn't mean it's obvious to everyone.

Keep reading – it's important stuff.

The IRS Didn't Call You

I'm leaving this in here from the other books because the scammers are going to use the new law to update their scams and make them seem even more believable. If someone calls with some scary new rule from the law, or some great deal from the new law that requires IMMEDIATE action from you – it's Bullcrap.

Unless you are currently involved in communications with the IRS that were initiated by you in person or by the IRS via a letter, that person calling claiming to be the "IRS" is full of you know what. The IRS does NOT initiate communications via phone calls. Scammers trying to steal your money or identity do. I have already had TONS of people (including a tax pro I work with) receive these kinds of calls. If you want a little more reassurance, try googling the number the call came from (if the number is hidden it's DEFINETELY a scam). Chances are the google results will be full of people asking about the number, and MANY people identifying it as a scam. If you want more reassurance, call the IRS (though this is pretty much a waste of time during peak filing periods.) These guys are professionals, and they can often sound very convincing, and will even threaten to arrest you. Swear at them and hang up.

UPDATE: They have gotten more sophisticated and are even sending relatively real-looking letters. Always assume someone calling and asking for money or personal information is a scam – tax based or not. Independently look the agency's contact information up online and call direct.

Have an Emergency Fund

I'm including this chapter from the other books because I just think it's critical in life.

This isn't really about taxes, except that a big tax bill is an emergency that would make having an emergency fund nice, and a tax refund is often the easiest way to start an emergency fund. Your emergency fund should be 3 to 6 months of living expenses. The cool thing about having one, is that this dude named Murphy, who has a law named after him, keeps track of who does and who doesn't have an emergency fund. Emergencies happen to people without an emergency fund, and generally don't happen to people who are prepared to handle them.

I told myself I need to expand this chapter to emphasize HOW IMPORTANT THIS IS…so…
Have an Emergency Fund.
Have an Emergency Fund.
HAVE AN EMERGENCY FUND!!!!

You should also have a budget, preferably one that has a budget item that puts money into your emergency fund at a rate that would refill it in 36 months or less. If it gets overfunded you can shift the money to something fun, but budgets keep your money under control, help avoid excess debt accumulation and let you plan for the future.

UPDATE: This revision was written in the midst of a government shutdown. These have become quite common. If you work for the Federal government or rely on it for your income, you are a fool if you don't have an emergency fund to protect yourself from it.

Update Your Address with the IRS and Your State

This has nothing to do with the new law, but is even more important with big changes since it's likely some people won't get the message on what's changed, and will thus be getting letters from the IRS. So…Update your address with the IRS…

EVERY TIME YOU MOVE! Believe it or not, the IRS doesn't automatically know that you've moved, and forwarding your mail is not reliable. The IRS sends letters to the address on your tax return if you haven't changed it. If the letter suggests a change to your tax return, the clock starts ticking on disputing it as soon as they send it. Updating the IRS when you move will save you a TON of heartache. This happens way too often, and is way too easy to prevent. Here's a link to an IRS site with more information: https://www.irs.gov/taxtopics/tc157.html. You're on your own for the state, but their Revenue Department website should make it easy.

This year I had three clients who were getting ID theft PINs from the IRS and didn't update their address. There is almost no way to fix this and avoid having to paper file.

Tax Software Sucks

This is even more true with a huge tax overhaul. The magnitude of programming changes and the timing of the law being passed almost guarantees things will be missed and the instructions for you will be confusing. They are not going to have a lot of time after the IRS finalizes the regulations to get their software right. So, everything I talk about below is going to get worse.

Why does tax software suck? Simple: it has to be both user friendly, easy to use, and accurate. If it's not user friendly and easy to use, no one's going to pay for it. Hell, that's why it's so popular! It is simply not possible to cover all the complexities of tax law and still be easy to use. So they make it easy to use: "How much did you pay for uniforms?" Sure, there's an info button you can click that will go into all the nitty gritty of this question, but if you read them every time they come up, it's not simple and easy anymore. "How many miles did you drive for business last year?" Again, many pop-ups will be available to help you navigate the dizzying rules that are involved in this simple question, but you're not likely to read them, and, if you do, they're only going to make you more confused. Don't even get me started on depreciation, business use of home, or investing income! And that's just the Federal return! Many states have nearly incomprehensible tax laws, and dozens of deductions and credits that you pretty much need to know exist in order to take advantage of them. Most software just drags things from the Federal to the State, with barely a peep about what deductions you might miss. I cannot even begin to describe the messes I've seen from tax software. Just this year, a client with one W-2, no wife, no kids, no house, and an amazingly simple Federal 1040EZ missed out on over $10,000 in state tax money over the last dozen years because either the software didn't ask, or he neglected to answer enough questions to establish that his military income was exempt from California taxes. Most of that money is gone forever. Tax preparation software SUCKS! You will have a better chance at an accurate return using pen and paper with the Federal and State instructions than you will using software!

My Other Books

If you like this book, you should check out my others:

Everyday Taxes 2018/2019 covers over 70 life situations with detailed information and advice in English. It is my most comprehensive (and expensive) tax book, but is indispensable no matter how you file. The idea is to be able to look up a chapter on what's happening in your life, see the effect on your taxes, and then take action to improve or mitigate the effect. I'm including a chapter list on the following page.

The Short Cheap Tax Book for Everyone is 50 plus pieces of advice that EVERYONE needs to know. Some of it is obvious (though ignored), some of it is obscure, but all of it is important (A small amount has been copied into this book).

I have several others, and am working on more, so keep an eye on my author page:

amazon.com/author/kirkea

List of Chapters/Topics from Everyday Taxes

1. Read Me First
2. Do I Have to File a Tax Return?
3. How Should I Be Preparing my Taxes?
4. How Much Should Tax Preparation Cost?
5. 10 Simple Pieces of Tax Advice
6. How Fast Can I Get my Refund?
7. Where's my Refund?
8. I Owe Taxes and Can't Pay
9. I Owe Taxes and Want to Get a Refund Next Year
10. I Get a Big Refund and Want a Bigger Paycheck
11. I Get a Big Refund, Is That Okay?
12. I Get a Big Refund and Don't Know What to Do with It
13. I Want to Lower my Taxes
14. I Can't File by April 15th
15. What's My Filing Status?
16. Can I Use Itemized Deductions ?
17. I'm Getting Married
18. I'm Having (or Already Have) a Child
19. My Kid's Getting a Job
20. My Child Had (or is Having) a Child
21. My Child is Getting Married
22. I'm Getting Divorced (or Already am)
23. My Spouse Abandoned me and/or our Children
24. My Spouse Died
25. I Inherited Money or Property
26. I'm Buying (or Already Own) a Home
27. I Made Home Improvements
28. I Made Energy Efficient Home Improvements
29. I Have to File Married Filing Separately
30. I Have Medical Expenses
31. I Have a High Deductible Health Plan and/or HSA
32. I'm Donating to Charity
33. I'm Living with Someone Who Helps Pay my Bills
34. I'm Supporting my Parents
35. I'm Supporting an Adult Relative or Friend
36. I'm Supporting a Minor Who is Not My Child
37. Someone Claimed my Child!

38. My Tax Return Got Rejected by the IRS!
39. I (or my Spouse or Child) am Going to College
40. I Have to Pay for Things for my Job
41. I Tele-Commute
42. I Work Overseas
43. I Lost my Job
44. I Had to Move
45. I Sold my Home
46. I Sold my Rental Property
47. I Sold a Home that Wasn't my Primary Residence
48. I Get Tips at Work
49. I Receive Benefits from the Government
50. I Have Investments Outside of Work
51. I Have (or Want to Have) Tax Sheltered Investments (IRA's)
52. I Want to Take Money out of my IRA or 401k
53. I Had Debt Written Off by the Company I Owe Money To
54. I Lost my House (Foreclosure, Short Sale or Bankruptcy)
55. I am Retired (or Thinking about it)
56. I am Retiring from the Military (Here Are Some Warnings)
57. I am Receiving Social Security (or Thinking about It)
58. I am Receiving an Annuity or Pension
59. I am Paying on Student Loans
60. I'm Changing Jobs
61. What the Hell is Alternative Minimum Tax?
62. I Sell Amway, Mary Kay, etc.
63. I'm an Independent Contractor or I Got a Form 1099-MISC
64. I Drive for UBER (or other cab like business)
65. I am (or will be) a Real Estate Agent
66. I'm an Artist (Tailored to Painters)
67. I'm Renting out my Former Home
68. What about the Affordable Care Act (Obamacare)
69. I Get Health Insurance Through the Healthcare Marketplace
70. I Don't Have Health Insurance
71. State by State Tax Guide for Military
72. The IRS Called and is Threatening Me!
73. I Got a Letter from the IRS
74. IRS Letter Types
75. I Got a CP2000 Letter from the IRS!
76. I Got this Form (look up forms you don't understand)

77. What about the Trump Tax Plan?

Appendix A - Support Worksheet
Appendix B - Insolvency Worksheet
Appendix C - Sample IRS Response Letter

54201334R00041

Made in the USA
Columbia, SC
27 March 2019